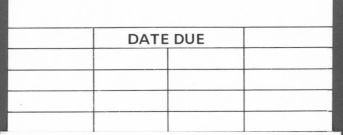

WHO ORDERED THE
JUMBO
SHRIMP?
AND OTHER OXYMORONS
JON AGEE

MICHAEL DI CAPUA BOOKS
HARPER COLLINS PUBLISHERS

OXYMORON (ok´si mōr´on), n.   **1.** an expression or figure of speech that combines contradictory or incongruous words, such as *guest host*, *a good cry*, and *gourmet deli*   **2.** from the Greek, *oxýmōros*, pointedly foolish [*oxý-* sharp + *mōros* dull, stupid] **3.** the inspiration for a goofy picture by Jon Agee

FREEZER BURN

CALCULATED RISK

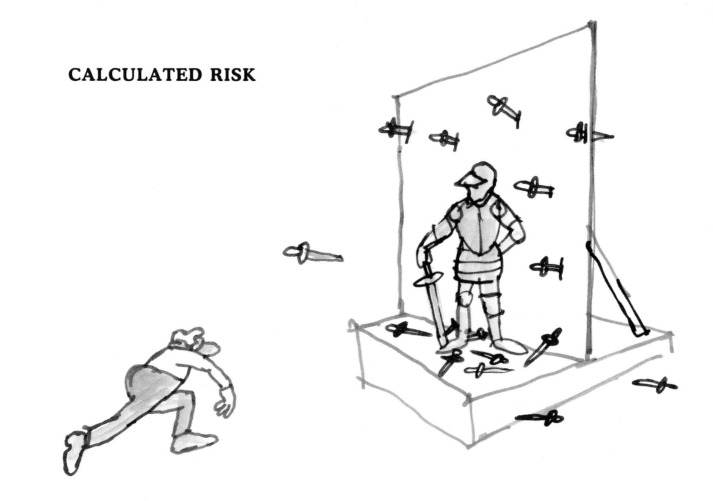

DRAG RACE

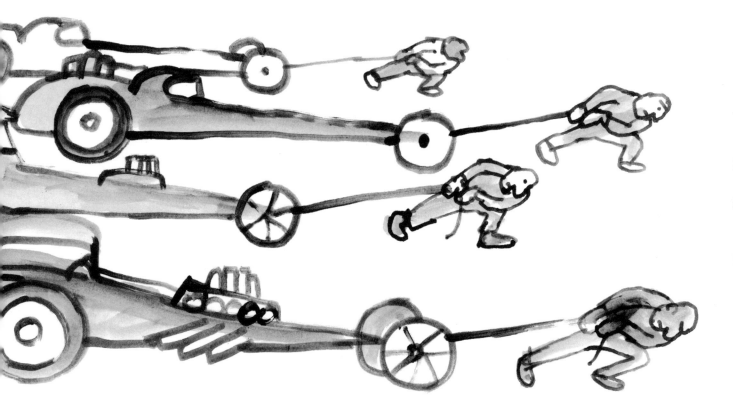

GENTLEMAN FARMER

BLACK LIGHT

SHARP
CURVES

SUN SHOWER

DAYBED

TOUGH LOVE

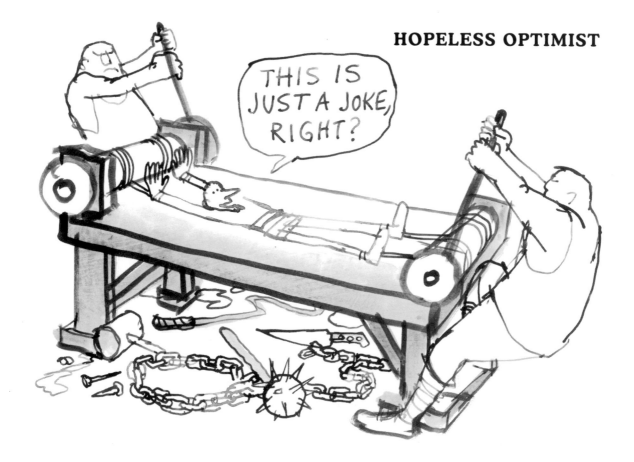

LIGHT HEAVYWEIGHT

WORKING VACATION

SMALL CROWD

URBAN COWBOY

COLD SWEAT

A LENGTHY BRIEF

LOUD WHISPER

ACCIDENTALLY
ON PURPOSE

THE ETERNAL MOMENT

BABY GRAND

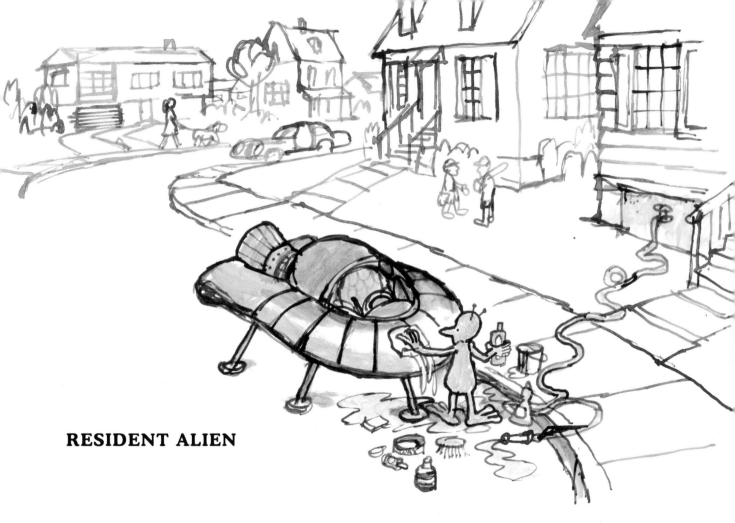

RESIDENT ALIEN

SUMMER SCHOOL

TERRIBLY CUTE

PRETTY UGLY

DRY LAKE

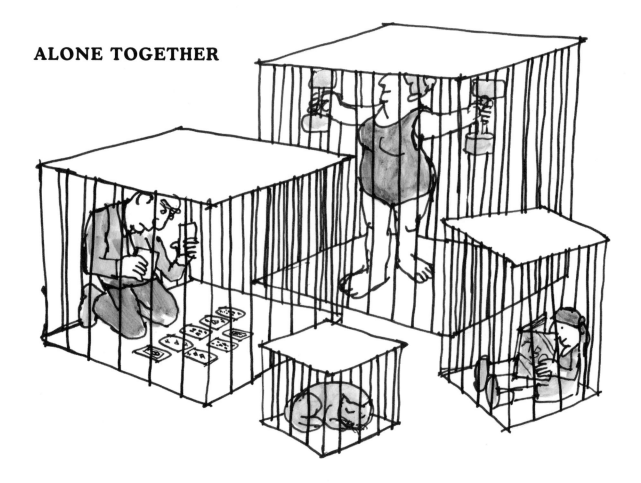

ALONE TOGETHER

SMALL MIRACLE

PASSIVE-AGGRESSIVE

POOR LITTLE RICH GIRL

THE GREAT DEPRESSION

DOWN ESCALATOR

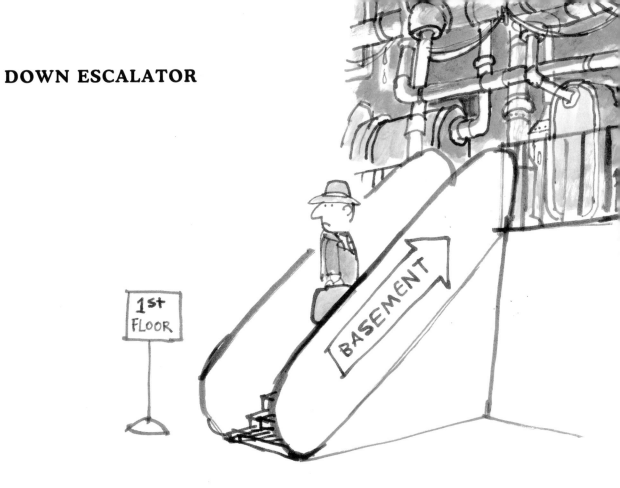

CONCRETE JUNGLE

GIRLY MAN

EASY PROBLEM

EVEN ODDS

INHERITED DEBT

ALMOST PERFECT

For Hope de Spair of Ocean Beach, Kansas

Thanks to Gary Bagley, Harry Baron, Tom Bassmann, John Baumann,
Liz Feigelson, David Feldman, Joosten Kuypers, Holly McGhee,
O. V. Michaelsen, Laura Olkowski, Glenn Pudelka, Annie Ravitz,
Eric Rockwell, Mark Saltveit, Will Shortz, Phil Warton, and Gilly Youner

Copyright © 1998 by Jon Agee
Printed in Hong Kong. All rights reserved
Library of Congress catalog card number; 97-78386
Designed by Steve Scott
6 7 8 9 10 11 12 13 14 15